About the Author:

Doug Mazeffa is the Research Director for Greenopia, the nation's premier green directory, and one of the leading experts on life cycle analysis and environmental impact assessment. Doug oversees all the various research products offered by Greenopia including its business, product, and corporate directories. Doug's environmental research has been featured in publications such as BBC, CNN, USA Today, CNBC, NBC, CBS, AOL News, The Economist, Huffington Post, Fox News, and other leading media outlets. Doug is also a highly sought after speaker including engagements at UCLA, UCSB, SF State University, SUNY Orange as well as numerous conferences, radio shows, and television appearances. Doug acquired his Master's Degree in Corporate Environmental Management from the Donald Bren School of Environmental Science and Management where he studied life cycle assessment, green markets, eco-labels, and consumer perception of the environment and completed his undergraduate work at Miami University. Doug currently sits on the board of the Clean Business Certification and Clean Business Investment Summit and is a judge for the Innovative Green Design Awards. Doug presently resides in Santa Barbara, CA.

Introduction:

Having worked in the environmental research space for many years, I find the amount of misinformation and confusion still surrounding environmental impact assessment staggering. Environmental impact assessment is a very complex field, not unlike that of ecology or engineering, but there is still a tendency for people to think that the solutions to environmental problems are obvious or that simplistic, single-minded product claims (recyclable, natural, organic, etc.) are guarantees that it has a lower environmental impact. This, however, is not always true.

The purpose of this guide is to provide readers with a thought process and approach that will help them truly determine if a product is green or not. Many of the principles in this text are rooted in Life Cycle Assessment and Industrial Ecology. You do not have to be an environmental expert to put these principles into practice.

In this text, we will discuss general environmental impact assessment, supply chains, materials, carbon offsets, and popular eco-labels and certifications. It is my goal by the end of this guide that you will feel much more comfortable going into a store and being able to determine which products are the most eco-friendly and do so with a higher degree of certainty. Although there may be 500+ eco-labels in the marketplace and dozens of buzzwords devoid of any true substance, it is important not to be intimidated or give up.

As consumers, we can have a tremendous amount of power through our shopping habits and if we leverage our purchasing to significantly increase demand for green products and services, the marketplace will have no choice but to transition into a more sustainable economy. Think of your shopping habits like voting. Although each individual vote may not appear to have substantial value, a large volume of votes in the same direction can influence the world. This is no different.

Glossary of Some Key Terms:

Eco-label – Any sort of environmental certification used (typically) for marketing purposes. Eco-labels are visible on websites, packaging, commercials, etc.

FTC – Federal Trade Commission. The agency that helps protect consumers from inaccurate and/or fraudulent advertising claims.

Functional Unit – The measure of the function of the product or service being studied. Think of it as the least common denominator (it terms of utility) between the two (or more) items being compared during a life cycle assessment. For example, you couldn't fairly compare a 20oz plastic bottle with a 12oz aluminum can. You'd have to normalize them so that they contain the same amount of liquid before doing the assessment (into 6 plastic bottles versus 10 aluminum cans, for example).

Impact Category – An environmental indicator (or indicators) being tracked in the Life Cycle Assessment. Typically, 5-7 impact categories are used in a life cycle assessment. Examples include Global Warming Potential, Water Consumption, Eutrophication, Smog Forming Pollutants, etc.

LEED – Leadership in Energy and Environmental Design. The leading green building certification developed by the US Green Building Council.

Life Cycle Assessment (LCA) - is a methodology to assess environmental impacts associated with all the stages of a product's life from raw material extraction through materials processing, manufacture, distribution, use, repair and maintenance, and disposal/recycling. It also typically involves tracking more than one environmental indicator throughout the various life cycle phases.

LOHAS – Lifestyle of Health and Sustainability. LOHAS refers to a type of consumers associated with a sustainable lifestyle. Typically LOHAS consumers are used to estimate the size of the green marketplace.

Willingness to Pay (WTP) – The amount an individual is willing to pay for a good or service.

Chapter 1 – The Successful Approach to Sustainable Shopping:

The first step in our journey is determining which type of environmental consumers we are. Although there are some definitions already in the marketplace (such as LOHAS consumers or naturalites), I prefer to think of this concept in terms of education level.

Consumers can be grouped in the following levels:

1. **The Naysayer:** A consumer that truly believes that the various environmental crises we are facing today are greatly exaggerated in spite of the overwhelming research findings and widespread adoption of environmental initiatives. Thankfully, this population is consistently decreasing and only represents a small percent of the public.

2. **The Traditionalist:** A more or less traditional consumer in terms of shopping habits, but one that still thinks the environment is important to protect because they see it mentioned in the news/media frequently. However, they haven't made much effort to green their lives or seek out additional information. I believe that most consumers fall into this category.

3. **The One-Trick Pony:** A consumer that knows the environment is important, but tends to think of these issues very simplistically or in terms of snapshots. For example, a person in this category might think that an organically grown product is better for the environment 100% of the time (regardless of any other attribute). I believe that most self-proclaimed environmentalists fit into this category.

4. **The Enlightened:** Someone in the 4th tier understands that environmental impact is a very complex issue, leading to some frustration or difficulty when making a purchasing decision. This person has made a significant effort in trying to understand the complexity of environmental footprinting and may even understand methodologies such as life cycle assessment. This person is very informed, but still may be missing a few key pieces of information. This group is made up of a small minority of consumers.

5. **The Green Guru:** This final group is made up of consumers who have made their peace with the complexities of environmental impact and understand that there are some basic patterns and thought processes to follow. People in this group may be confident enough in their education level that they can even make environmental choices

that reflect specific environmental preferences (such as favoring water or toxicity issues). Very few consumers ever make it to this level.

It is my goal through this text that no matter which level you currently reside, that by the time you finish you are at the very least the 4th tier, and hopefully the 5th tier. It is my belief that no matter what your current education level, if you are open-minded, you can walk away from this book with a lot to consider. I would also encourage you to seek out additional information, especially some of the groups that I site throughout the text. There is a 'Further Reading' section included at the end of the book.

Life Cycle Assessment:

In my opinion, the single best tool in determining environmental impact is called life cycle assessment or LCA. LCA is a very complex methodology in which you look at a series of environmental indicators (typically several around resource consumption, water pollution, and air pollution) throughout the product's material extraction, manufacturing, transportation, packaging, usage, and disposal. This approach gives a much more complete picture of the overall environmental impact of a product versus a traditional carbon footprint (which only tracks emissions) or supply chain analysis (which doesn't include the use phase or disposal of the product).

Any environmental expert will tell you that LCAs are tremendously complex. I have worked on LCAs for rather straightforward product types that still take 6-12 months and millions of dollars to complete. But, even as a consumer with limited information, you can still make the basic principles of LCA work for you. Here are the main principles to take away from LCA to help decrease your personal environmental footprint while shopping.

1. **Start to think about products in terms of their overall life cycle and not just one life cycle phase.**

   One of the questions I get asked the most frequently is "Which is better, organic or locally produced food?" The answer I always give is 'it depends', because with that little information, making an informed choice is impossible. Furthermore, organic and local are not mutually exclusive. It would be better if the item was both, but it's also worth pointing out that in some extreme cases a product could actually be worse for the environment by being organic and/or locally produced. In general, try to stay away from these simplistic claims and instead focus on the bigger picture, including whether or not the region it was grown/made in is climatically and ecologically suited for its production, how it was packaged, etc. Beware of a product that only has one environmental attribute worth touting, unless it is one of the few product types (like vehicles) where one part of its life cycle (in this case the use phase or fuel economy) is responsible for almost its entire impact.

For example, let's consider an organic cotton T-shirt. Organic cotton is touted as a green fabric by just about every major clothing manufacturer. And while it is fair to say that organic cotton is better than traditionally grown cotton, I'd argue that it is far from one of the greener fabrics. All cotton production (organic or not) is incredibly resource intensive and is one of the biggest water/land hogs of any fabric. When you conduct a LCA comparing organic cotton to other green fabrics such as tencel, hemp, jute, capilene, etc., it performs rather poorly. In fact, organic cotton doesn't even perform that well relative to polyester. For reasons such as this, be careful of any environmental buzzwords, especially ones that pertain to a very narrow window of the products life cycle.

2. **Don't just limit your environmental thinking to only one impact area.**

This is another dangerous tendency that is common in the marketplace. It is very possible that a product could emit 10% less carbon dioxide equivalent than another product, but still be worse in terms of its other resource consumption and pollution metrics. The organic cotton T-shirt example from above is relevant here as well. According to a LCA conducted by researchers at Tampere University, organic cotton performs about twice as well as polyester in terms of energy consumption, but consumes over a thousand times more water. So just because it does better in terms of emissions, is it really better for the environment overall? Don't just limit your thinking to one environmental area because you can very easily be misled.

3. **Try to figure out where the biggest impact areas are in terms of the different life cycle phases (material, manufacturing, transportation, packaging, usage, and disposal).**

Although this may seem tricky at first, it shouldn't be surprising that for vehicles and electronics, that the use phase (essentially the energy that it needs to be powered on) is typically the largest contributor to its environmental footprint. Likewise, for food items, it shouldn't come as shock that the production, packaging, and transportation typically play the biggest roles in its impact. What this comes down to is really trying to visualize what goes into the product and, from that, being able to estimate what the footprint of the product will be as a result. Anything requires power to use will always have a substantial use phase impact and the more basic the product, the more important impacts such as packaging and transportation become.

4. **Make sure that when you study two products in terms of their environmental performance, that it is in fact fair to compare them head-to-head.**

In LCA this is process is called determining a 'functional unit' for comparison. For example, it's not really fair to compare a standard aluminum can with a standard plastic PET bottle. This is because they hold different amounts of fluid (12oz and 20oz, respectively) and therefore the products have a different overall utility from the consumer's perspective. The best way to compare such a product is to pick a unit that they both fit evenly into, such as the consumption of 120oz of beverage, which would then pit 10 aluminum cans against 6 plastic PET bottles. Such a step ensures that the comparison is as fair as possible.

With these basic LCA principles, hopefully you can begin to see that although impact assessment is a complex issue, there are still some basic principles that you can arm yourself with to make better decisions.

So then, how do you use this information while shopping in order to have the most positive impact possible?

1. **Consider the type of product you are buying and if the environmental claim/attribute even matters.**

   Some of the funniest things I have seen in my various roles are the claims that companies try to get away with. A few of my personal favorites include a small store who tried to promote that they now used lead-free paint (can you still even buy leaded paint?) and I cannot even tell you how many companies use 'recyclable packaging' in their marketing materials. In this day and age, most packaging is recyclable and these groups should be focusing on packaging minimization, post-consumer recycled content, or alternative materials.

   What's amusing about these types of claims (besides how generally pathetic they are) is that in terms of the overall environmental impact of the product or service, they don't really matter at all. This is a common ploy used by many different types of companies, but is very notable in electronics. Remember to always think about what is important in the life cycle of the product and if a company is solely touting an area that only represents a few percent of the product's total impact, be very wary.

I've noticed a trend that people naturally tend to over-value packaging, transportation, and disposal of products. I am in no way trying to say that these are not important in their own way, but in many of more complex product types (electronics, vehicles, appliances, etc.), they typically only account for 2-3% of the total life-cycle impact of the product at most.

Don't fall into the various PR/advertising traps set by many companies. Figure out what matters the most for this specific product type and make your decisions around the top performers in those areas.

2. **Just because the product has an eco-label or certification does not make it automatically better for the environment.**

This is the subject for the next chapter, so I won't get too granular here, but don't assume that just because the product has some sort of special marking with a green tree or a happy butterfly that it is necessarily better for the environment. As of this writing, Ecolabel Index reports there are over 400 eco-labels in the marketplace. I have also some seen some estimates that puts this number over 500 labels in the US alone. While on average an eco-label on a product is a good thing, there is enough greenwashing in the marketplace to ensure that you should make an effort to understand what an environmental certification means before completely trusting it.

The FTC is starting to crack down on these certifications and labels, but realistically it will be decades before the market will be completely safe for consumers to trust.

3. **Use the best possible resources to make an informed decision.**

Although the amount of information required to make a good green choice can sometimes feel crippling, the good news is there are many resources that you can utilize for help. One of the best groups that has a number of incredible consumer resources is Environmental Working Group. Their cosmetic database is, in my opinion, the best-researched resource for any beauty or personal product. Two other very good groups to gather information from are the Organic

Consumers Association and the Organic Trade Association. Both of these groups have taken a lot of action to make sure organic claims are more credible and meaningful. Finally, and admittedly a bit of a self-promotion as I do work for them, I would recommend checking out Greenopia. Presently, Greenopia is the largest local green business directory in the US as well as the leader in corporate environmental ratings. If you are curious how various major brands stack up from an environmental standpoint, check their data out.

4. **If you know the materials from which a product is made, you can usually get a sense of its impact.**

Having a sense of how materials typically perform when compared to one another can be a very useful way to determine which product is actually greener. In general, the best materials to worst materials are, in order, recycled content (any), biomaterials, paper, plastic, glass, aluminum, and then other metals. Although this is not true in every sense, it is a good starting point. Also, keep in mind that less of one material type might be needed during manufacturing versus using another. For example, to make a beverage container, less plastic will always be needed than glass because of its material characteristics. Therefore even if the two materials perform approximately the same environmentally, you might only need a small fraction of one of them to complete the production cycle which would make it the optimal choice.

When in Doubt, Logic it out:

One thing I always try to make clear when conducting workshops is that, although environmental impact itself is very complex, most people already have a very intuitive sense of what has a big impact and what doesn't. For example, if I were to show you a piece of paper and a sheet of aluminum that are the exact same size and asked you which had the bigger environmental impact across its life cycle, you would almost certainly guess that the aluminum sheet had the bigger impact.

If you think about it logically, paper is produced from harvesting wood and is pulped down and processed, where it eventually becomes sheets of paper. Aluminum, on the other hand, starts out as bauxite ore, has to be extracted from the earth and then refined into Alumina using very high temperatures and lots of energy. Even without going into detail about the supply chains and material flows, it should be clear that paper production is less environmentally damaging than the extraction and refinement of a metal.

Another example is if I were to ask you which vehicle had the bigger environmental impact to manufacture, a traditional SUV or a conventional sedan. The answer to this question should even be more obvious. All you really have to think about to figure this out is the amount of material they each contain. A sedan may only have a curb weight of 3,200 pounds whereas an SUV could easily weight up to 5,000 pounds. Since vehicles typically are made from very similar materials or technologies (and in the same relative proportions), it is safe to say that the larger vehicle (essentially the one made with more material) has the bigger production impact.

In some cases, you can also use prices to your advantage as well. In general, products with higher prices (i.e. luxury products) tend to have a bigger impact. For example, if you take two similar sedans, one being a base model economy sedan and the other being a high performance vehicle, you can safely surmise that the luxury vehicle is going to have the bigger impact. Even ignoring the fact that luxury vehicles typically get dismal mileages, they are also going to be made with more electronic components and materials like hardwoods and leathers which have a bigger footprint than the cheap plastics used in economy vehicles.

The same logic holds up fairly well for other goods as well. Products like clothing, furniture, and electronics can follow similar price-impact patterns. But, I should warn you, that personally I do not like to solely rely this price-based thought process as there are too many exceptions and I find that this metric isn't really that scalable (meaning there is no real value in computing an exact impact per dollar because of the generalizations that must be used). It certainly something to consider when making a purchasing decision, but I would be a little careful when making big choices using just this one approach.

Keeping Social Indicators in Mind:

Although I am a huge supporter of utilizing a life cycle methodology like the one outlined above, I would feel terribly guilty if I didn't discuss one caveat about the approach. At this point in the book, you may be noticing that there is a distinct focus on environmental performance and not very much mention of social, economic, or political indicators. This is very much by design. Although LCA is starting to incorporate some social and even economic indicators, there are some issues in doing so.

At a very high level, it should make sense that comparing environmental indicators to ethical ones is problematic at best. Environmental indicators are designed to quantitative and can be very precise in terms of their impact. The production of a computer will have a certain amount of energy, emissions, water, waste, etc. associated with it. This is not the case with ethical considerations which tend to be much more qualitative.

There are tons of clever ways to include economic/ethical data in an LCA (wage data, employee happiness, living conditions, job creation, etc), but these indicators mean different things to different people. In one person's mind, it might be very valuable for a company to utilize unionized labor and they may have solid arguments for doing so, but talk to another person and they may have valid arguments against such an initiative. Another example could be tracking employee satisfaction or even the satisfaction of the consumer using the product. However, satisfaction is going to mean different things to different people.

The same can be said for health effects at both the production and consumer level. At the production level one might track a metric like injuries or accidents. Organizations like OHSA make such data available for any consumer who is interested. But, the reporting of such events is treacherous because what really defines an injury or an accident? Some workers may be prone to report issues while another may not. Therefore you might conduct such an analysis and come to a misleading conclusion.

From the consumer health/safety perspective, it can be very difficult to link adverse effects directly (and conclusively) to a single product or service. Just imagine trying to develop a study to determine if organic food was actually healthier than conventionally-farmed food. To have a truly useful data set, the researcher would have to account for every lifestyle variable to ensure that other causes didn't influence their results, not to mention have a true control population. There are statistical methods to try to account for this, but the studies are still problematic at best.

I want to point out that the above commentary is in no way to discourage people from looking at social indicators or trying to develop better approaches. It is simply to ask you to be cautious when applying the same thought process to something as readily quantified as a water footprint against how a product impacts a culture or a human life. We all know that issues such as wages, child labor, and human rights are tremendously important. I think by trying to simplify and quantify such values, we run the risk of cheapening and distancing ourselves from the problem at hand.

Chapter 2 – Navigating Eco-Labels and Certifications

One of the most difficult parts of being in the environmental space is keeping track of the hundreds of eco-labels and certifications that are in the marketplace. Some of these labels are legitimate, while others are less rigorous, and there are even some that have been developed to blatantly mislead consumers.

First off, let's consider the current status of eco-labels and green certifications. Eco-labels constitute more than a billion dollar sector of the economy and there are presently hundreds of labels available. Eco-labels are also not a new phenomenon. The first official eco-label was Blue Angel in 1978 and the first in the US was Green Seal, which was created in 1989. But, it has really not been until the past 10 years where the marketplace for eco-labels has taken off.

At best, eco-labels have a mixed response in the marketplace. On one hand, numerous studies have showcased a higher consumer willingness to pay (WTP) for certified green products or services. One needs only look to the considerable popularity that organic products have achieved in the past decade to see that this higher WTP exists. And since consumers have this expressed and quantifiable desire for such products, it is fair to say that there is indeed some value to these labels.

However, this is not to say that the average consumer has any idea what the labels actually mean. With the exception of USDA Organic and Energy Star, very few (if any) other labels have consumer awareness level over 50%. Furthermore, a lot of the awareness statistics are collected and analyzed by the labels themselves, presenting a bit of a conflict of interest. But even if the awareness levels were somewhat higher, being aware of the label is still not the same as understanding what it means. If we assume that for any eco-label that half of all shoppers recognize the label, what percent would be able to actually explain what goes into the certification process? Probably very few.

One of the most common presentations I give is about the 20 most visible/notable eco-labels in the US and what they actually mean in terms of impact assessment. My favorite exercise at workshops is to have participants keep their hands in the air as I show them the top 20 labels until I come to one that they do not recognize. After 6 years of this exercise, the most any audience member has ever recognized is 12 of the 20 certifications, and the average is only between 2 and 3.

Businesses, on the other hand, tend to have a critical view of eco-labels, largely due to the difficult process they must go through in order to be able to achieve any such certification. A study completed by Jay Golden at Duke University in 2010 showed that on average it took 4.33 months for a product or business to be certified. To a small business owner, that is an incredibly long time. To be fair, the study also showed a very high standard deviation in certification completion time. Although in my experience, the certifications that are very easy to go through also tend to be the least credible and are the same ones not readily recognized or embraced by consumers.

Another barrier to eco-labels on the business front is the cost of obtaining the certification. The typical eco-label will cost a business between $2,500 and $25,000 depending on the certification type and the size of the operation being certified. There are also annual fees associated with most certifications. Also keep in mind the costs in terms of time commitments and any additional staffing or any back-end changes that have to be made, including machinery, lighting, materials, etc. The time commitment alone can be considerable depending on the certification type and may require lots of documentation such as utility bills and supply chain credentials.

Finally, eco-labels are suspect in the eyes of business owners in terms of their return on investment (ROI). If a business is going to invest a total of $10,000 into a label, they want to see that money returned within a reasonable timeframe, hopefully with additional revenue coming in.

Certain certifications have clear ROIs, such as LEED, which will pay for itself through lower utility bills, but it is less clear whether seeking a label such as USDA Organic or Fair Trade is always a good business decision. While obtaining certifications such as these will give you access to a new audience of consumers (with a higher WTP), typically the costs of production will also have increased which cuts into the company's margins. Although I am a fan of both USDA Organic and Fair Trade, there have been times as a consultant I have recommended that I client not pursue such a certification because it clearly would not be the best action for their business. After all, it is important to remember that a business-owner can exceed the criteria of any eco-label in existence, but not actually apply for such a seal.

So then, as a consumer, what are the important aspects of the environmental certification marketplace and what should they mean in terms of your shopping decisions? The answer is that eco-labels can be your best friend while shopping, if you learn the basics about what goes into a certification and think about what they are tracking.

The first step to understanding eco-labels and the role that they play is to list the attributes that would be required to create a credible and relevant certification in the marketplace.

The considerations you would want to see in any seal would be:

1. **A comprehensive set of criteria that have been developed by unbiased experts and tested in the marketplace and are relevant to the goal of the label.**

   You'd be surprised how many labels fall short of this basic principle, something which seems should be the cornerstone of the entire eco-label marketplace. Some claim to have a message of sustainability, but have generic criteria that do little to move the ball forward. It still amazes me that there are certifications out there that use a standard like 'the farm must utilize sustainable practices whenever possible'. What does that even mean?

   You should also be careful about labels that have been developed by the industry that it is trying to regulate. There are some cases where the labels can be relatively rigorous in spite of this conflict of interest but, more often than not, the purpose of an industry-developed label is to give its members a very quick way to market to green or ethical consumers.

2. **Some sort of auditing process to ensure the businesses actually follow through on the certification procedures.**

   To be fair, this is actually a lot more difficult than it seems. Sure, it is common sense to have someone audit the business/product before allowing them to utilize their certification seal, but the implementation of such a system can be tricky. By requiring audits, thousands of dollars are added onto the certification cost that the manufacturer has to pay to complete the process. Interestingly, the same 2010 Duke study by Jay Golden I mentioned earlier found that only 53% of labels require field audits and only 76% require any form of data audit at all.

3. **Formal update process for the criteria and methodology of the label.**

   I cannot state how important this is. LEED is a great example of how to do this correctly. Since its creation in 1998, LEED has gone through numerous iterations. Other labels have a tendency to come up with a standard and then never change their system even when better information/data becomes available.

Because environmental impact assessment techniques are really just starting to come into their own, it's important to have some flexibility built into your model or you risk becoming irrelevant as better science becomes available. Energy Star is unfortunately an example of a certification in which many of its thresholds are relatively obsolete (although it has other points of merit). Also, because Energy Star is a pass/fail standard (as opposed to one like LEED that has different levels of certification achievement) it becomes hard for a consumer to make a meaningful choice when they go into a large electronics store and the majority of the products available seemingly have this certification.

4. **Transparent claims about the environmental benefits of obtaining the certification versus the status quo.**

This is another item that is tremendously important. If you can't easily find out what the standards of the label are, or if its claims are ambiguous, it might be suspect. Although standards for many of the leading eco-labels can be well over a hundred pages, the main characteristics of the labels should be able to be summarized in a page or two (and typically are somewhere amongst their available materials). If you are checking up on a label and can't clearly find out what it is tracking or what the specific benefit is supposed to be, be very wary of it and consider pursuing a different label.

5. The label has a credible group behind it.

Ideally, you would like to see an NGO or government body behind a label such as Organic (USDA), LEED (USGBC), Energy Star (EPA), etc. By having such a group behind it, you can feel more comfortable that it is a credible label and that there are enough resources (both mental and physical) to ensure that it has a rigorous vetting/research process. Certifications that do this avoid two problems. The first problem is if there is a group behind the label with a clear agenda that is not conservation-minded. This can happen when a label is powered by an industry trade group, for example. These certifications can exist solely to confuse consumers or to make companies look like they are good environmental citizens when they are in fact not.

The other pitfall is labels that are generic such as 'natural' or 'biodegradble'. You will see these terms on products, but they are actually not certifications in the truest sense of the word. Instead these are simply marketing claims that may or may not be accurate. As I mentioned earlier, the FTC is cracking down on these claims, but it is still going to take time for the market to sort itself out.

Eco-Labels and the Marketplace:

Now, let's consider the actual current marketplace for eco-labels and certifications. Of the desirable traits we just listed, I would estimate that only the top 5% of eco-labels meet all five criteria. Let's then assume that there are approximately 500 labels in the marketplace. This then means that there would be about 25 credible environmental certifications out there. Such a high percentage of junk eco-labels in certainly troubling, and you might wonder why the marketplace has gotten to such a point where the vast majority of the labels are useless.

The first explanation for the sad state of the eco-label marketplace is simply that its complexity makes certifications much more difficult than say 'quality' or tracking a certain product performance aspect (like a 0-60mph time). Environmental labels have to consider a wide range of impacts typically across several life cycle phases, so in order to make the process efficient and not charge companies hundreds of thousands of dollars in certification fees, everything has to be somewhat scaled back. Compounding this is that few companies, if any, actually track every single environmental metric with any certainty. Therefore how is an outside body supposed to regulate and certify a business that doesn't have perfect data, and in some cases couldn't even if it tried?

For example, consider USDA Organic. Organic is a credible label for sure and, as a consumer, you can be assured that if you buy a product with the USDA Organic seal on it, it's actually going to be organic. USDA does a phenomenal job checking up on the farms and ensuring that they have been organic for at least the 3 years that is required for the certification and is very picky about the other inputs that are used. But, even though USDA Organic is certainly a credible label, as we discussed in the first chapter, it's not necessarily always optimal for the environment. There is a whole gamut of environmental and agricultural practices that Organic certification does not consider and therefore should not be a simple substitute for meaning a product is green. This is not an attempt to undercut USDA Organic as a label, because I firmly believe that is has a tremendous amount of value, it's just often frustrating that a complex issue such as environmental impact has been incorrectly reduced to one word in the eyes of many consumers.

The other issue facing eco-labels is that environmental impacts vary widely industry to industry so groups tend to only focus on one or two product types. Consider the two most widely recognized eco-labels, USDA Organic and Energy Star. Organic is limited to food products, fabrics, and beauty products, while Energy Star is limited to electronics, appliances, and buildings. And, the funny thing is, relative to the rest of the certification marketplace, they are actually pretty dynamic. There are countless labels that just apply to just to one product type like coffee, wine, or even flowers.

So what are some shopping tips you can follow to help navigate the various environmental seals that are out there?

1. **Be conscious of limitations of seals that only focus on one impact or life cycle area.**

   USDA Organic, Energy Star, CarbonFree are all great labels, but they have very distinct limitations. They are often great starting points for products or services, but ask yourself if they adhere to all the principles discussed in Chapter 1.

2. **Educate yourself about the lesser-known labels that actually take a life-cycle approach.**

   Lost in the midst of hundreds of questionable labels are some really strong standouts. The labels I always point consumers towards that are the most thoughtful, credible, and complete include Green Seal, Cradle to Cradle, EPEAT, LEED, Biodynamic, and Direct Trade.

With the exception of LEED, a very small percent of consumers will be familiar with any of these certifications. Help support these groups who are going the extra mile by purchasing the products they have certified.

3. **Likewise, educate yourself about some of the more questionable eco-labels that appear in the marketplace.**

   Just like there are some incredible labels worth touting, there are also some that are not as rigorous. In general, tend to be wary of certifications that are for-profit or run by industry trade groups that have a clear agenda. Also, be careful of seals that are just a marketing ploy as opposed to having an actual organization behind them. Some terms and seals to watch out for include Natural, Recyclable, Biodegradable, Rainforest Alliance, Naturally Sephora, Nontoxic, and Free-Range.

4. **Find resources to help you make more eco-friendly shopping choices.**

   For eco-labels in particular, one of the best resources in my opinion is the Eco-Label Index which is available online. It can be accessed at www.ecolabelindex.com. This resource provides information for over 400 eco-labels and tracks what they are, who runs them, and data about the certification process. To see the bulk of the data there is a fee, but even the free information provides a good amount of insight for concerned consumers. Also, when in doubt, a simple Google search can provide a lot of good information about the label or seal. You should be able to figure out the basics of a label in 5-10 minutes of searching online.

The future of the eco-label marketplace will be very interesting. Between the FTC crackdown and consumers becoming more and more informed about environmental impacts, I suspect that the marketplace will be very different for eco-labels within the next decade. Only time will tell if this change is for the better or worse.

Chapter 3 – Considering Tradeoffs and Assessing Environmental Impact Data

Now that we have gone through the basics of life-cycle assessment (LCA) and eco-labels, it is time to move on to arguably the most important aspect of impact assessment: Tradeoffs.

In one form or another, everyone is familiar with tradeoffs as part of the decision-making process. However, in the environmental field, tradeoffs can almost become paralyzing. For example, let's say that I produce a beverage and through whatever means, I learn that there is a 1 in 100 million chance of my product causing cancer each time it is consumed. Even though the number may seem small, let's also say I have a supply chain magnitude the same size as Coca Cola. According to Coca Cola's website, 100 million cans doesn't even represent a full day's sale. Now all of the sudden hundreds of people are getting sick each year because of something wrong with the use phase of my product (i.e. the consumption), so I certainly need to do something about it.

Let's also say that the issue turns out to be the way that a particular ingredient interacts with the coating used in the aluminum can. Once I learn this, I put my best scientists on the job and they are able to use a substitute material so the cancer rate from consumption drops from the original

1 in 100 million to 1 in 1 trillion. At first glance, this seems like a positive outcome of altering the supply chain, right?

The truth is it's not that simple. It's quite possible by taking that approach (which is a tremendously common and even logical thought process) that I have not only made the product's total impact higher, but I even could have indirectly made the overall cancer rate worse than what it originally was.

Unfortunately, the decision is not as simple as just replacing the coating or the material that needs to be coated. It's possible that by making the switch in the supply chain the largest cancer risk now shifts to a different life cycle phase. For example, let's say that in the old supply chain that the majority of the manufacturing and material acquisition took place in an area with very clean energy such as California. However, because of the change we made in the supply chain, now the manufacturing utilizes a much dirtier energy grid mix (because we had to use a different factory for the new manufacturing process which happens to be in a place like Ohio). Dirty energy generation produces chemicals like cadmium, arsenic, lead, and mercury, which have huge cancer risks.

Given our enormous supply chain, all of the sudden we might be causing a whole gamut of health problems (not to mention spiking any other environmental indicators) simply because we tried to make one part of our production process less toxic. So in this example, the health problem would shift from the use phase to the manufacturing phase and we could have a situation that is an overall negative from where we started even though we may have looked like we addressed the problem.

The above example is in no way to discourage companies or individuals from trying to improve the impacts of their products or services. But, it is to serve as a cautionary tale that having good intentions and trying to make something better/safer can lead to disastrous results if the process is not thought out properly. This example is also not to make you think that behind every action is some disastrous unforeseen consequence. As the next example illustrates, sometimes the opposite can be true.

I wish I could remember where I first heard the following story because it has served me well over the years. When I first heard it (sometime around 2006), the original author of the story maintained that it was a true happening from their past days as a supply chain researcher.

Their client (a tool manufacturer) was attempting to green their operations as well as trying to find ways of lowering their manufacturing costs. For their drill line, they wanted to see how much the average customer utilized the drills before disposing them in the hopes that they could create a recycling or take-back program and be able to reuse some of the internal components to aid in their production. In order to figure out this metric, they embedded a device in some of their drills that monitored its usage and then when the drill was collected at its end of life they could see the amount of time it was actively used before disposal. Before I reveal what the reported value ended up being, think to yourself how many hours you think the average consumer actively uses a drill (i.e. the drill bit is spinning) before throwing it out and getting a new one.

Have a guess?

The answer is only on the order of 10 or so minutes.

When I first heard this number, I was shocked. First, because I felt somewhat misled by the question asking for the answer in terms of hours, but also because that seemed like a small amount of time for an electronic device to be used before being thrown out. But, then I really thought about it. Thus far in my adult life, I have owned 3 different drills and with the exception of some furniture assembly or picture hanging, they have never been used. Such a device only being used 10 minutes by the average consumer seems completely plausible.

This finding had several ramifications for the tool company. The first was rather than focus on a recycling program and trying to implement the used components, the company could actually use less durable (and less impactful) materials to manufacture parts. There is no point in making a product last for 500 hours of continual use if it's almost never going to be used even 1% of that time. This means that coming out of the manufacturing facility, the impact of the redesigned drills would be substantially less than the prior models. This also led to savings for the company as their material costs decreased significantly from the substitution. Presumably, they could also lower their product's prices to consumers to attempt to increase demand for their products as well.

Therefore you can see that tradeoffs can cut both ways in terms of looking at altering various life cycle phases. But, it's also important to consider that tradeoffs can also occur between impact categories (i.e. environmental indicators) in supply chains as well.

Again consider a beverage container. Let's assume that there are five possible material types from which a beverage container can be made and still have identical utility and performance in the eyes of a consumer: steel, aluminum, plastic, glass, and a paper carton. If I was to conduct an LCA of these materials (and I have) and were asked which one I would recommend from an environmental perspective, I could honestly reply that I would recommend the paper carton. However, this is not to say that the paper carton is the best for every supply chain or that it performs the best in every environmental indicator. Tradeoffs exist in terms of these areas as well.

Once I have selected a material, I'm going to have to pick a supplier or factory to manufacture the containers. Based on the location, technologies that are used, and even their local utility provider, the answer might not be as clear as just picking a material and sticking with it. Each selection is going to have a resource efficiency across different areas (waste, water, energy, emissions) and very rarely does one perform better in every single one of them.

Remember that although materials are great starting points when conducting an assessment, they don't always tell the entire story.

Likewise, even assuming an average supply chain, the materials themselves are going to have different environmental attributes and it is very rare that one material excels in all of the indicators you are tracking. Paper cartons might do very well in terms of energy efficiency and toxicity, but might score towards the bottom in water consumption. Plastics may score fairly well on energy, water, and emissions, but be the worst performer in toxicity.

Such cases are tremendously common and should not be met with panic. Here are a few tips:

1. Don't be afraid to assign weights to the various environmental indicators. Although care must be taken that these values are not totally arbitrary, treating them all as equal can be problematic as well. Also consider the data gaps or confidence intervals that surround each indicator. Whereas values for energy, emissions, and water are usually fairly precise, indicators such as eutrophication, toxicity, biodiversity, etc., might have much more uncertainty surrounding them.

2. If a technology, material, or product is scoring better in a majority of the indicators you are tracking, it is probably safe to recommend. The exceptions to this are if the product is only scoring more favorably by a very small margin and is worse in the other areas by a huge amount or if the product is performing very poorly in an area that you care about substantially more than the others.

3. If a technology, material, or product is scoring significantly higher in a few areas, but slightly worse in the majority of the indicators, it might still be the better selection depending on how important you are weighting those indicators.

4. When in doubt, it is always good practice to conduct a sensitivity analysis on your model. This

will show you how much your model is impacted by changes in your assumptions.

Sensitivity analysis is a tool of which every impact assessment expert should be aware. One of my biggest criticisms of the many LCAs that are in the marketplace is either that a proper sensitivity analysis was not conducted or that the authors downplay just how susceptible their findings are to changes in a few assumptions.

The goal of a sensitivity analysis is to gain an understanding of how vulnerable the findings of your model are to changes in your assumptions or modifications to the supply chain. For example, a product may show that 60% of its overall impact is in the manufacturing phase because of the energy required during this phase. Looking at the study, it turns out this value was derived from the assumption of using the US average energy grid mix (meaning the average energy source breakdown of the US as a whole) in the analysis. In most cases, this will be a poor assumption. Most goods will be produced in specific states or areas with grid mixes very different from the US average. For instance, if I were to plug in a California grid mix, the value might drop from 60% to 20% given California's cleaner energy profile than the US average. On the other hand, if I were to plug in Ohio's (or some other coal-dominant state) it is quite possible that number could grow from 60% to 75% or even higher. In this case, the results would be hyper-sensitive based on this one vague assumption which makes the study questionable in terms of decision-making.

Another common example of the importance of sensitivity analysis is with the transportation phase of the product. If you just put averaged data in the model, it can be off by an order of magnitude. Likewise, knowing the exact percentages each transportation type used (truck, air, boat, rail) will give a much clearer, although still incomplete picture. What often makes transportation one of the trickiest areas to precisely quantify is that it's not just as simple as plugging in the transport type and mileage. You also should consider how full the vehicles are during transport, return trips, and vehicle efficiency (at least to the best of your ability).

In general, the less precise the data is, the less valuable the study is in terms of making a truly informed decision. The best way to avoid sensitivity issues is to use as much primary source data as possible. At the end of the day, if you know the actual values, utility providers, etc., the findings should better reflect the real world.

Impact assessment is really about making decisions with incomplete information that doesn't always perfectly align. You have to be comfortable enough with your models and data when making a choice, but the important thing is that better data is always becoming available and, as such, you should frequently update your assumptions to make sure it reflects the best science available.

Chapter 4 - Carbon Neutrality, Renewable Energy, and Carbon Offsets

At this point, there is a pretty strong, if not irrefutable, case for human-influenced climate change. If you still firmly believe that human activity is not impacting global climate, then you have a remarkable ability to be able to ignore a staggering amount of evidence, most of which has higher certainties than areas such as medicine, nutrition, etc. Currently, just about every major corporation (even companies like Exxon) is making changes to meet current or potential climate legislation. This is taking a few different forms.

One example is the 35 US states (as of this writing) that either have Renewable Portfolio Standards (RPS) or Renewable Portfolio Standard Goals. This is a fancy way of saying that these states have some sort of renewable energy target by a certain year. They vary state to state, but common goals are using 20% renewable energy by 2020 or 25% by 2025. Obviously, the hope is that by switching to a substantial portion of renewable energy, that we can lower our carbon dioxide output and start to mitigate our effects on climate change. What is interesting, though, is that there is no consistent definition for renewable energy between the states.

ClimateCentral has a very useful and interactive map of the each US State's RPS (if the state has one) available on its website. By clicking on each state, you are taken to the government website that outlines the RPS standard that is in place. I encourage you to spend some time playing around on this because the different definition each state uses for renewable energy is staggering. Ohio, for example, even includes a form of nuclear power in its RPS. When you take into account the different technologies that are possible to include in each RPS across the US, you have almost a dozen different technologies.

I suspect that most consumers would find this surprising because we typically think of renewable energy as either solar, wind, geothermal, tidal, and hydroelectric power. For the most part, these are proven technologies in terms of overall environmental benefit. Now, all of the sudden, projects such as biomass, nuclear, waste to energy, coal-fired gasification, and others are eligible to be part of the standard. This should be at least a little alarming.

While it is normal to expect deviation in terms of what energy types are being used because of geographic viability, some of these are a little bit ridiculous. Nuclear, coal-gasification, and some forms of biomass have no right being called renewable energy. But, what does all of this mean in terms of your shopping and personal lives?

The big take-away is if you are either looking at getting renewable energy for your house or you see it on a product label, go the extra mile and see what type of renewable it is. It's actually very easy to find what types of energy you are sourcing from your utility provider, and likewise it's usually pretty easy to track down the renewable-type when a claim is being made by a product. If you are unable to find the exact renewable being touted, it's definitely cause to be wary.

A good rule to follow is that the following renewable energy types are positive:

- Solar
- Wind
- Geothermal
- Tidal
- Small-Scale Hydroelectric

Likewise, the energy types listed below can be positive, but it depends on the exact process and the ways in which they are utilized.

- Biomass
- Waste to Energy
- Landfill Gasification
- Large-Scale Hydroelectric

Finally, the energy types below should in no way be considered renewable or green.

- Clean Coal
- Cogeneration
- Coal Gasification
- Nuclear
- Any Other Fossil Fuel

Another related area where there is a lot of misinformation in the green space is the carbon offset marketplace. Out of the 200+ industries I have studied in my career in terms of legitimacy, impact assessment, transparency, and consumer perception, carbon offsets are one of the most abstract and complicated. This is a shame, because I truly believe that carbon offsets can be a very valuable tool, but for every group that is credible, there are a few that are either out to make a buck, or have no idea what they are doing. If you closely monitor offset providers, it's a bit shocking how quickly some go under and how many have popped up in recent years. There are definitely some mainstays, but it's a transitional sector to say the least.

There are a couple of important concepts you have to understand before you can begin to assess carbon offsets. The first is the difference between a Renewable Energy Certificate (REC) and a carbon offset.

The big difference is that RECs revolve around carbon mitigation as opposed to sequestering existing carbon (like an offset does). The idea behind a REC is that a company or individual pays to be able to say that they source renewable energy. The certificate that you are provided for this purchase acts as proof that this renewable energy process actually took place.

Carbon offsets involve a more deliberate action and actually removes carbon dioxide equivalent from the atmosphere. Examples of some types of carbon offsets include reforestation, methane recapture, and truck fuel switching. All of these examples will remove or prevent carbon dioxide equivalent from being released into the atmosphere in real time. But, carbon offsets are also held to a different (and arguably higher) standard than RECs. Most offset standards have what are called additionality criteria.

Additionality is a scary sounding term, but the notion is just that an offset must prove that it wouldn't have taken place unless the consumer or firm actually paid for it. Essentially each purchase allows for an 'additional' sequestration of carbon dioxide equivalent based on the size of the sale. Seems pretty straightforward, right?

In practice, however, additionality can be a bit murky. Right off the bat, renewable energy types cannot really be offsets, because they are going to operate whether or not a consumer buys from them.

Deciphering Carbon Offsets:

Are all carbon offsets created equal? The answer is a resounding no.

There is still a lot of debate as to which offset types are the best. A good offset should have several characteristics. The first is that it should actually have the desired effect of sequestering carbon dioxide equivalent and do so in a reasonable timeframe (i.e. 1 year). As mentioned before, it should also meet additionality criteria. The carbon offset should also be measurable and audited in some way. And, finally, the sequestration should be permanent.

The most controversial carbon offset types are typically reforestation and avoided deforestation projects. Let's go down the list of desired traits and see how they stack up. Do they have the desired effect: yes. Is it done in a reasonable timeframe: it could in theory, but many reforestation offsets allow for 100 year time periods. Do they meet additionality criteria: yes. Is the sequestration measurable: sort of. This can be done on an averaged scale, but is ultimately going to vary season to season and tree to tree. Thus, beware if the reforestation offset uses the same number across the board for the life of the offset. Finally, is the sequestration permanent? The answer to this is no. Once the tree dies (or God forbid if there is a fire), the carbon is just released back into the atmosphere. Therefore reforestation and avoided deforestation is a stop-gap offset at best.

To be fair, there are other benefits that these offset types can have that other projects do not. For example, assuming the reforestation isn't a homogenized tree farm, reforestation can help bring back biodiversity to an otherwise denigrated landscape. These projects can also have social and economic benefits (such as increasing land values) and many of the certifications for reforestation projects focus on these areas. So, when making your choice, you have to ask yourself which is more important, the offset having the exact desired effect or that it could lead to some other positive outcomes that might not be possible through other offset technologies.

One of the other popular offset types that better holds up to scrutiny is methane recapture. The basic idea behind methane recapture is relatively simple. Since methane has approximately 21 times the global warming potential (i.e. climate impact) of carbon dioxide it is important to capture and remove. Methane is a natural byproduct of decomposition of waste and organic matter. As such, devices are built to essentially capture the methane and turn it into carbon dioxide which is much less impactful. This process also typically has the benefit of being able to generate energy as well.

So how does this system stack up to the characteristics we outlined? Does this method have the desired effect: yes. Is it done in a reasonable timeframe: yes, typically less than a year. Does it meet additionality criteria: also, yes because these devices would not be built otherwise. Is the sequestration measurable: yes, as we know the global warming potential of both methane and carbon dioxide. Can it be done in a reasonable timeframe: also, yes. Finally, is the sequestration permanent: also yes, because the gas is changed into a less impactful one as a result of the process.

Therefore, as the above illustrates, methane recapture fits the bill across the different characteristics that one should look for in a carbon offset. But, as I noted above, this method does not necessarily have the same positive ethical and biodiversity effects that a landscape method may have. It's really hard to say whether one is better than the other, but if all you are worried about is the actual sequestration then you are probably best served by staying away from forestation carbon offset projects.

In terms of shopping influence, one of the most common ways you will see offsets and RECs in the marketplace is companies claiming to be carbon neutral. Obviously, no company on the planet can actually provide their good or service without having some impact, so this neutrality is coming from the offsets or RECs described above. When you see such advertising angles, make sure they are not just offsetting the production impact or one area of their supply chain. You'd be surprised how many companies will word the claim such as 'carbon neutral manufacturing process'. This may lead you to believe that then the product has a net climate impact of zero, but in actuality the company might only be offsetting a fraction of their total footprint.

So is this a claim that we as consumers should value? Personally, I do give such claims some credence, but given the inconsistency of the offset marketplace, it's dangerous to delude ourselves into thinking that a carbon neutral product is actually 100% carbon neutral. The good news is that such claims are being heavily scrutinized by the FTC and the marketplace should get more and more credible each year.

Based on my research, here is a rough breakdown of how the various carbon offset types stack up in terms of actual mitigation potential.

Good Offset Projects:

- Landfill Gas Capture
- Farm Gas Capture

Typically Good Offset Projects (Depends on Exact Case):

- Fueling Switching
- Renewable Energy
- Fuel Efficiency

Questionable Offset Projects:

- Reforestation
- Avoided Deforestation
- Soil Management

Chapter 5 - Bringing It All Together

With the information in the previous chapters, you should hopefully have a good foundation to know how to approach shopping decisions in the proper environmental mindset. Although impact assessment is certainly a technical science, there are still ways you can arm yourself with basic principles and make the most ecologically friendly decision most of the time.

Although there was a lot of information in this guidebook, there are several important takeaways that if you forget everything else in this book I hope you remember and utilize. These are listed below.

1. Consider the impact of the product or service throughout all of the various life cycle phases (material acquisition, production, transportation, packaging, use, and disposal) as opposed to just focusing on one.

2. Remember that typically for durable or complex goods, transportation, packaging, and disposal have a very modest (at best) impact on the environment. This is not to say that these areas should be ignored, but you will be better served focusing on the other phases. Likewise, for simple goods like food or beauty products, packaging and

transportation can be very significant chunks of the impact.

3. Likewise, the use phase tends to be the most important for any sort of electronic. This can range from 40%-50% of the impact for items like laptops to over 90% of the impact for items like refrigerators or light bulbs.

4. Certifications can be a good starting point when assessing a product, but remember that most eco-labels are questionable at best and tend to be very limited in scope. As such, stick to the most researched and credible labels.

5. Be wary of products that are touting suspicious or potentially misleading environmental claims. If the most notable claim of a product is that the packaging is recyclable, then there is a good chance it's not doing much else to be green.

6. Always keep in mind the materials from which a product is made. If you know the material types and their weights you can usually get a solid feel for the environmental performance of the product.

7. Remember to consider the tradeoffs of a product or service, but don't let it paralyze you into not being able to make a decision. If you are

considering two different products, and the only difference between them is the material from which they are made, think about how each material impacts the environment.

8. It is important to remember the limitations in all assessment methodologies. Although environmental impacts may be well defined, they often ignore ethical issues. It is also worth noting that ethical metrics are not as readily quantified and teased-out as environmental ones, so be a little careful when looking at studies attempting to track ethics in a very precise sense. Ethical concerns are always going to mean different things to different people as well.

9. There is a distinct difference between carbon offsets and Renewable Energy Certificates (RECs). Carbon offsets actually sequester existing carbon dioxide equivalent while RECs are simply mitigations efforts.

10. Not all carbon offsets are created equal. A good carbon offset has to meet additionality criteria, be measurable, permanent, completed in a reasonable timeframe, and actually have the desired sequestration effect. If an offset you are considering does not meet one or several of these criteria, then it's probably not worth buying.

One final thought:

The turning point for me pursuing a career in the environment was an article published in the journal *Nature* by Robert Costanza in 1997 that discussed a valuation of what are called ecosystem services. Ecosystem services are the benefits that nature provides for mankind that allow us to survive such as soil formation, water filtration, air purification, etc. What was so amazing in my mind about this study was that these services, which we often take for granted, were estimated to have a value of $33 trillion dollars per year. That is not a typo, I meant to write trillions. By comparison, and as of this writing, the GDP of the entire world is just over $11 trillion. This means that nature provides services that have a value three times higher than everything humans produce on the planet combined.

Consider that for a second.

Obviously we need the natural resources the planet provides to make just about everything, but isn't that still a sobering statistic? Even if Costanza's estimate is off by a considerable amount, we should never forget that every product we use and every luxury that we have is because of natural resources. If we exhaust these resources, there is no telling what is in store for us, but it's safe to say that it won't be pretty. At the end of the day, we have to stop being so short-sighted and think long term. Sustainable business is good business and if we don't start changing our behavior now, future generations will undoubtedly suffer. Being green is not that difficult and it doesn't require a huge lifestyle change. All it really takes is being smarter about what we do and how we approach our lives.

Thank you for reading.

Acknowledgements:

First off, I would like to thank my beautiful wife, Lauren, for putting up with me (most of the time). She's always tremendously supportive of my endeavors and this text was no different. I would also like to thank my friends, family, and colleagues for your support as well as a great resource from which to bounce ideas. I'd also like to point out the hard work of several groups that I have mentioned in this text. Environmental Working Group, EIA, EPA, US Green Building Council, the Bren School at UC Santa Barbara, and the Nicholas School at Duke are all great resources and extremely credible organizations and groups. I'd also like to thank Greenopia and its staff for its hard work and also as a resource. Finally, I would like to thank you for taking the time to read through this (and for actually reading the acknowledgements). The goal of this text was to give you some of the tools to being to lower your impact and I hope it achieved that goal, but I cannot discount that your willingness to go along for this brief journey and learn something was crucial. Never forget that your actions have repercussions and the amount of influence that consumers hold over a market can be staggering.

Further Reading:

Below is a list of groups or studies I have referenced throughout the text. Check them out for more information.

www.climatecentral.org

www.eia.gov

www.epa.gov

www.ewg.org

www.greenopia.com

http://www.nmisolutions.com/index.php/syndicated-data/segmentation-algorithms-a-panels/lohas-segmentation

http://www.organicconsumers.org

http://www.ota.com/index.html

http://www.usda.gov/wps/portal/usda/usdahome?navid=ORGANIC_CERTIFICATIO

Costanza, Robert *et al.*, "The Value of the World's Ecosystem Services and Natural Capital". *Nature*, Vol. 387 (1997), p. 259.

Golden, Jay et al., "An Overview of Ecolabels and Sustainability Certifications in the Global Marketplace". Retrieved at http://center.sustainability.duke.edu/sites/default/files/docu ments/ecolabelsreport.pdf. October 2010.

Kalliala, Eija, et al., "Environmental Profile of Cotton and Polyster-Cotton Fabrics". *Autex Research Journal.* Vol 1 (1999), p. 8-20.

McCluskey, Jill et al., "Consumer Preferences and Willingness to Pay for Food Labeling: A Discussion of Empirical Studies." *Journal of Food Distribution Research*, Vol 34 (2003), p. 95-102.